Sallie Durham

I Left My Hair in San Francisco

Indigo Dreams Publishing

First Edition: I Left My Hair in San Francisco
First published in Great Britain in 2022 by:
Indigo Dreams Publishing
24, Forest Houses
Cookworthy Moor
Halwill
Beaworthy
Devon
EX21 5UU

www.indigodreamspublishing.com

Sallie Durham has asserted her right under the Copyright, Designs and Patents Act 1988 to be identified as the author of this work.
© Sallie Durham 2022

ISBN 978-1-912876-67-9

British Library Cataloguing in Publication Data. A CIP record for this book can be obtained from the British Library.

This book is sold subject to the condition that it shall not, by way of trade or otherwise, be lent, re-sold, hired out, or otherwise circulated without the author's and publisher's prior consent in any form of binding or cover other than that in which it is published and without a similar condition including this condition being imposed on the subsequent purchaser.

Designed and typeset in Palatino Linotype by Indigo Dreams.
Cover design by Ronnie Goodyer at Indigo Dreams
Printed and bound in Great Britain by 4edge Ltd.

Papers used by Indigo Dreams are recyclable products made from wood grown in sustainable forests following the guidance of the Forest Stewardship Council.

For Zhenya

ACKNOWLEDGEMENTS

Love and thanks to my family, friends and mentors who gave me green lights when I was stopped at a red.

Thanks also to the judges of:
The Plough Poetry Prize (*Other People's Lives*);
The Bridport Prize (*I Left My Hair in San Francisco*);
The editors of The New Writer magazine (*Festival* and *Light*).

Warmest thanks and gratitude to Ronnie and Dawn for allowing my poems into the light.

"Tomorrow, and tomorrow, and tomorrow" (*Optimism*) was borrowed from *Macbeth*.

CONTENTS

I Left My Hair In San Francisco 9
Other People's Lives 10
Festival 11
Light 13
Under A Lincolnshire Sky 14
Debussy 15
Whisky Mac 16
Vigil 17
The Messenger 19
Ma's Cook Book 20
Ladders 21
Finland 22
On Sketching The Arbousier Tree 24
La Météo Marine: A Warning 25
Teenager On Holiday 26
In Petrozavodsk 27
Bubbles: On Meeting Our Russian Daughter 28
The Seagull 29
The Relocation And Care Of Goldfish 30
The Bullocks Next Door 31
The Cranefly 32
Meditation, Last Day Of Summer 2020 33
Walking Through Clouds 34
Snowdrops 35
Death Of A Juvenile 36
The Humming 37
Iris 38
A Fever Of Sunflowers 41
Lockdown Holiday 42
Sunflowers, Saumur 43

Life Of Clytie 44
The Psychology Of Sunflowers 45
The Evening Primrose 46
The Russian Giant 47
Miss Happiness 48
Old Sunflowers 49
Sunflowers In October 50
Optimism 51
A New Wood Pigeon Tries Her Wings 52

I Left My Hair in San Francisco

I Left My Hair In San Francisco

You want haircut? Long pretty hair, nice.
Twenty two dollar I tidy-up, yes, thirty
dollar for you, I wash hair please, you sit
here. Where is parting? Where you from?
You live London? London nice. Queen
nice lady. I cut here? I take this much.
I go snip-snip, I make you nice pretty hair
for holiday. You love jewellery? Nice
jewellery next street, pink store, you
buy something pretty, ok? I go chop-chop,
nice bob, look pretty. You want me cut
bangs? You want see eyebrow? I cut bangs
straight across. I go hack-hack, look nice,
look ten year younger. You have child?
Why you no have little boy, brother for girl,
play together, nice, you want me dry hair
straight or curly? I dry curly, look nice,
won't see hack-hack when curl under. I take
thirty six dollar for tidy-up, look rubbish,
I take dollar, I spoil holiday with bad haircut,
I go hack-hack, I give you terrible theatre wig,
I turn you into Richard the Third, I make you
cringe at reflection, I make you wish you not
come in, I make you wish you walk past window,
past tattoo boss man rolling bad cigarette,
past my dirty scissors going snip-snip chop-chop
hack-hack –
I make you wish you keep walking, not stop,
keep long pretty hair for holiday.

Other People's Lives

You could tell by the way they walked
keeling to one side, like boats, or drunks
something was wrong.

His eyes were dead as pebbles.
The shuffling woman beside him
wore the same granite look
though she found a light to smile by.

Only their black-and-white mongrel dog
radiant and straining on a long, blue leash
seemed to know where they were going.

Festival

The sun was seductive that day
Luring us out of the shadow of an accident.
We followed drums to the churchyard
Transformed overnight to a movie set –
Mad fish in cages
A cellophane spirit like a blue wave between leaves
An owl, so delicately woven to a rowan
You couldn't tell which was which
And among the graves were plaster lice the size of rugby balls.
Morris dancers came in a Christmas cacophony
Scarlet streamers sweeping stone walls
Fiddle and accordion telling of medieval antecedents
While the African drums summoned
A picnic of chicken, rice and beans.
At the marine exhibition
We examined the sliding doors of the mouths of crabs
Touched anemones like beetroot.
A man with a stutter showed us
The lobster's regenerating claw
Swirling at its side like a slip of silk.
On the houseboat – half a coach stuck on the starboard
We gazed at giclée pictures
Helen's hats and Hamish's toes.
Our daughter played on the bungee.
A clumsy mummy hurled her child too quick
And the waiting children fell like skittles.
And though we felt the shadow of Daddy's accident –
Hospital wards, the recovered mountain bike
Festival held it off.

Evening, I surfaced in heels
To savour paintings, to slowly sip Prosecco.
Our little girl, elegant in handkerchief dress and fluffy mules
Went tripping past the jazz trio on her way to the loo
A miniature lady with a toy racoon –
She drew every head towards her.
Talk turned to accidents, the death of a photographer
So we ran away to the cellophane spirit
The mad fish, the owl, and the giant lice
All alive in starlight.

Light

That's me in the photo,
my eight-year-old self
caught in a fall of honeylight,
bracken to my waist and
the black trees a conspiracy
of witches.

Go and stand there, Dad said,
and I became this photo, and then
I became another –
my short bright hair
lamping St Peter's porch,
arms thin as a grasshopper's.

A stolen day of light,
me in my gingham schooldress
and my dad, released from work
rolled up his sleeves, took up his camera,
did the job that God always
meant him to do.

Under A Lincolnshire Sky

Under a Lincolnshire sky
sour wind is binding ivy
to the pear tree.

Three fuschias have made it
to February – redundant children
on the frozen motherbush.

My father is curling in upon himself,
a question mark –
how did I get to be so old that I must
scythe myself upstairs?

Head down sideways on the table,
hands starfished on ashy wood,
listening to Rachmaninov.

Debussy

The clouds continue to bank
their platinum.

He's sitting at the kitchen table
steeped in *Clair de Lune*
and cigarettes.

Mauve smoke gathers in corners –
how long since he looked at the sky
or even wanted to?

Whisky Mac

I was barely off the bus
and he'd ask me –
Did you bring the Crabbie's?

My father's house could be
muffled in dust, but in certain things
he was exacting –

two parts whisky,
one part Crabbie's,
I was always on the rocks.

Later, when the whisky mac
didn't mix with co-codamol,
he'd instruct me in the preparation
of a fizzing medicinal cocktail

two parts cold water,
one part hot water,

then I'd carry it over
proud as anything
sometimes with a red straw, or blue

and those were the times
I'd hear him say, *There's a good girl.
There's my favourite daughter.*

Vigil

The early call and the mercy dash.
Train – coffee – train – coffee – train – train – bus.
Red leaf, yellow berry, red leaf, yellow berry,
giddy fish in the slipstream of emergency.
Red berry, yellow leaf, red berry, yellow leaf.
Lonely panic of heels and wheels.
In his kitchen, three witches in a death-spell.
The repositioned bed, and my father not my father
but a giant white-beaked bird, eyes receding
in the viper-sweet release of morphine dreams.
Instructions to cancel the papers,
cold tea vacuumed through a straw, his request for bread
a pearl of hope, of life reversing,
his mouth a flattened and colourless 'o'
shaping Sinatra.
Curtains open. Curtains closed.
The failing songs and the sealing eyes.
Night nurse with the marigold hair,
Tap-tap-tap of death watch knitting.
The guilty hours of a ravaged sleep.
Light on, light off. Curtains open.
Nurses, and the bamboo-thin of him,
that Bowie song, *you don't eat when you live too long.*
His one hearing ear a well of love and memories.
My half-done prayers.
On the chair, my book winged up like roadkill.
Unfinished crossword wanting ALFALFA.
Redundant shirts hunched on the line.
Violet flatworm of patchouli incense.
Mozart taking him out on the trippy golden stairway.

Terrible quiet of a stopped heart.
The ironed skin and the sour sheet.
Tenor of blackbird
through an open window.
Yellow berry. Yellow berry.
Red leaf. Red leaf. Red leaf.

The Messenger

Grandma knitted out her final summer
casting off in shapeless yellow yarn
the exact colour of rapeseed,
no one asked what she was making.
The house took on the dull cosy hush
of the sickroom, the walls so steeped in sadness
even the cats were depressed.

When combine harvesters came to chew the wheat
I ran through stubble and the ragged flames
of poppies, exploding pheasants left and right,
red-and-green screaming fireworks.
The stubble was a nest of needles
on which I slept, then woke to a violet sky
and a compulsion to look behind
into the eyes of a hare, quietly nibbling.
A cold stare shiny as buttons.

The world stopped. The hare stilled.
A raindrop pierced my arm –
and in an arc of feathered air it was gone.
In its bristling space, our cottage
my mother and grandmother standing side by side
like witches at the window.

Going in as the storm broke
they said how they'd willed me to turn around –
how I'd felt the pull of ancestral mothers
as surely as if the earth had opened up
and their muddy hands had reached for me –
nameless, faceless women claiming me for kin,
the hare trapped between us,
a messenger.

Ma's Cook Book

All the best recipes were in her
little brown book, with the
stained cover like a map of Africa.
Banana bread and devilled chicken,
the trifles she assembled –
glazed cherries, and the upflung
arms of ghost-green angelica
were tiny drowning men in seas of cream.

I don't know how she found the time
to write them down, those flawless
pencilled loops, rubbed to crumbs
by a decade in a dark drawer –
secreted away like love letters.
Every recipe a rainy afternoon,
a kiss, a glimpse of lifting elbows,
hands gloved in gunk, her laugh.

Ladders

A sit-and-think seat, and a cloud for a hat.
My thoughts arrive clear as sapphires
on the tainted breeze.

We were blown away in a sweep of old leaves –
where have all the good years gone?

O paint us a sky of pink promises
and we'll do our best to keep them
even when you're darkly and squarely
turned from me, and I'm at the end of my
promontory.

Nothing divides us, but gold-lit doorways
and fathoms of light and dark.
Can we return to those dazzling stars
we knew at the start? Are there too many
ladders – can we climb them again?

Only think of her, in her parallel world
of soft dangers. She'll fight her corner
with three sets of dice, she's a gothic princess
stranded.

It's nighttime. The raven is watching.
The book is open at the middle of our lives.
The moon is pinned to a tree.

Tell me, my love, can we coax roses
from barbed wire?

Finland

Just me and this oak tree, spine against spine,
the message I cannot send –

What was that thing
       you wanted to tell me?

And was there ever such a sky of clouds
puffed up like giant popcorn?

Do you remember
       how we talked about Finland?

On and on about Finland.

Finland this, Finland that,
our voices sinking
       lower, deeper
unable to find the bright words
to lift us
       out of darkest Finland.

Do I know this thing
       like
a bee coming at me in a bullet of truth,
a blissed-out honeybags, missing the point
       entirely
slamming into bark.

I would have called you sooner, but
       where were you?

Did you hide away
        because of that thing
you wanted to tell me?

I wish I'd waited long enough to listen
        not sting the conversation

for fear of getting stuck inside
        the honey of your words.

What was that thing you wanted to tell me?

On Sketching The Arbousier Tree

This tree seems all elbows and knees.
It reminds me of us.

Arterial branches bleed
towards all that is forgiven.

I have tasted the honey of the dark red fruit –
it snares and divides me.

My pencil, rising through bark and leaf
is trying to reach you.

La Météo Marine: A Warning

Le mercredi she's going to be *agitée*
thrashing her hands, a woman demented,
by midi becoming *forte* –
and she'll be looking for things to throw

exhausted by le jeudi, *peu agiteé*,
all her minions still cramponed to rocks.

Le vendredi finds her *belle ou ridée*
a dancer spreading her turquoise skirts
smiling like it never happened.

Le samedi, all ready for l'amour.
Le dimanche, le lundi, le mardi
peu, peu, peu agitée.

Teenager On Holiday

The restaurant is a glass box on stilts
with a view of veridian smoky peaks.

She's weeping over the French menu
and everyone is speaking fucking French.

The *civet de sanglier* sounds disgusting.
Her *soupe paysanne*, when it arrives,
is a fucking swamp.

So we get her this Corsican fucking salad,
which is a salad of meat and cheese
and quickly pilfered while she's
scowling into the strawberry sunset.

And all she wanted was the little pizzeria
she'd seen across the street –
anything, anything that isn't fucking French.

In Petrozavodsk

Outside my window
the pink neon lights of Hotel Sayonara
come unthreaded in snow.

All along Prospeckt Karla Marksa
and down to the lake,
trees begin to yield their scratchy backs
to cribs of tender green.

My heart is breaking
for the child I haven't met.
If I could hold out my arms to her –

she will be made of ice, and snow,
and a Russian sunrise.

Bubbles: On Meeting Our Russian Daughter

the
first bubble
grew like a pear
sagged and vanished
you were sternly
unimpressed

the
second bubble
neatly launched and
full of plump possibility
exploded on a
stone post

the
third shaped up
like a Fabergé egg
of swimming rainbows
and then your finger
shattered
it

you
stepped back
from the next big
bubble with a look of surprise
wiped the wet lick
from your nose
and how we
laughed

finally you smiled.

The Seagull

Hates my husband.
A shouty entity with shopping bags.

Now she waits for him
on her rainy corner
of bluesky mornings and
dogbark afternoons
her silver eye
piercing the night.

When he walks to the shops
she is waiting
with her nasty laugh
a hunched, mad weathervane
screaming down like a missile
from one end of her world
to the other.

She's the worst kind of seagull,
vengeful and spiteful
razoring neighbours' cars
pulling feathers in the playground.

Walk away.

Walk three different streets
and let her consider:
harmony of blackbirds
fellowship of trees
generosity of clouds.

The Relocation And Care Of Goldfish

In my life there were goldfish – the ones you win
at the fairground; goldfish that no one wanted,
bug-eyed and bellowing in a plastic bladder
instructions we could not understand.

If your goldfish survived its transportation
it would be siphoned into a jam jar
while you searched for a glass bowl, or
if it was lucky, an entire tank
with pink bridges and emerald weeds
like mermaid hair, and then it could dine –
but anyway
you would have acquired goldfish food
like potted coloured dandruff
with a smell of fish paste.

You might have wondered why the fairground
folk never gave to you the smallest morsel
to help with the relocation and care of goldfish
who might have grown up eloquent,
and not be found bent and rotating in their
salt-or-hairspray-or-cigarette-polluted home –
how I cried for Skipper, Frisky and Carrot.

In my life there were tinned peaches,
fast swimming in waterfalls of slimy syrup
to a cut-glass bowl my mother would offer
for dessert
which no one wanted, like the fairground goldfish.

After their moment of glistening orange glory
it was downstream all the way.

The Bullocks Next Door

All summer the bullocks leaned
over the fence to take from me
tiny apples in their plastic noses
and though I crossed the field at a safe angle
we knew of the other's presence,
never meeting –
until my torchlight uncovered
a shuffling brotherhood
of shining eyes and blue breath.

The next day they are gone
and the empty field is a country
whose people have fled –
the big clouds herding fast
across a bloody sky
of abattoir thoughts.

In their hay-sweet side of the field
in the hoofy mud and
the fly-hungry dung
they will come to sit in the sun again
a magpie on the beige bullock's back,
untouched by weather or
emotion – and somehow
I envied them.

The Cranefly

A cranefly is dying on the bathroom window,
a rusty nail attached to wires –
and with a mechanical pulsing
he punches tiny careful holes in the steam

trails a morse code of dots and lines
into a vague painting of a quadruped.
Maybe in this weird death dance he has
discovered genius –

with these six feet I could have been Maradona.

On the next pane he makes a steam-printed perfect heart –
what, did you imagine craneflies don't feel love
for their multitudinous cousins and brothers
all so creepily identical …

did you believe
they had no ambition and were content merely
to hang from ceilings like empty nets
hell-bent on your face in the middle of the night …

If you have wondered sometimes
what is the point of craneflies
be sure he's thinking this too

slumped down on the windowsill
his last two fingers up in a V.

Meditation, Last Day Of Summer 2020

Because Amber said, why don't you come along,
and so did Joss.
Because the sky was a black sieve of silver holes.
Because a canteloupe moon was in the sky.
Because they said to bring a blanket and I wanted to
wrap the whole of summer in it.
Because the curlyheaded motheroak spread her arms
above us.
Because I opened one eye and everyone was breathing.
Because the owl transmitted love from his heartface.
Because the moon had slipped behind the motheroak.
Because a sisteroak had died and was making art
from her own dead limbs.
Because inside a corona of fairy lights craneflies were
frantically excavating the meaning of life.
Because my unwrapped legs were cold as winter.
Because all we can hope to do is breathe. One breath,
and then another.
Because the moon sailed off like a kite and the oak tree
was sighing to be left alone.
Because we cannot meet like this again in case we
kill each other.

Walking Through Clouds

Up on Black Cap I've lost my path
in a panic of yellow fog –
my cloudy signpost skews away
to an altered world.

Maybe I'm no different from
these sheep
teetering on the blade
of a steaming volcano.

Here on the crest of the bostall
a kestrel is holding the air
in his windy hands –
he has made from his tail
a death-fan of chopsticks.

I walk down to the valley of trees
immobilised in frost like a beautiful virus;
comes a sound like igniting paper –

the trees are sloughing sugar cubes
and grains of rice
and under the lifted fog
a brilliant village of snowdrops.

Snowdrops

Here you are again
igniting our corners.
It's not that we didn't expect you –
rather, you were gone so long
that you took us
by surprise.

Let me see you –
green-inked, three-winged,
secret as the moon.

You have been patient,
biding your time in a long,
dark sleep we can only imagine,
awaiting your turn to shiver
in the cold sunshine
of the young year.

Such a short time you have,
gone before tulips
lost in lavender –
and in the autumn
we must be careful
not to wake
the sleepy nubs of you.

Death Of A Juvenile

A young blackbird
hangs his chimes in the ash tree.

Still high on music,
he enters the garden –

out of the hyacinths
a trap of claws

perforates the aria
that was forming,

leaks his lifework of songs
to the mute soil –

inside the soil
the broken featherwork of him,

grey bending shadow
of a bluebell –

the ash tree hushing notes
in the blue morning

and through the blue
afternoon

into bled dusk.

Inside her cage of blossoms
his mama is fussing so.

The Humming

Old Mother Blackthorn
has lifted her snowy arms
to the spring sky
so that on the third day of March
a hundred bees are humming –

queen bees, queer bees, trans bees
and all the key worker bees
released from icy prisons
to a sudden pollen party –

humming, humming, humming
humming, humming, humming

mantras of anticipation.

Iris

Because she dares to wear
an extravagant satin gown
they believe she's fair game
for defamation;

she stands accused
of hogging the rainbow,
of consigning to shadow
those who love sunlight

and muting those
whose voices are colourless
when she dares to speak
in tongues of purple.

She can take it all,
human admiration, the kiss of a cat,
tuning out the nayers and haters
with her radiant silence;

she will have her fill of youth
and praise and notoriety,
her one yellow eye marking
time as frantic as leaves

as urgent as dragonflies
and the wild dances of bees
and the hurtling blossoms
and the sly fingertips of flowers

already reaching up
to silence and displace her,
begging their turn in the garden;
have they forgotten

what she'll become –
victim of her own thirsty purple
lifting her parched mouth
to the inevitable stream

and on her sunken lovely face
a cobalt cicatrice,
that unexpected smell of meat
recalling the lives of women

our weeping and our bleeding
disguised in fine attire –
not these paper collars
scratching our necks.

Too soon she'll become
something other –
briny and olive like toads
with an ammonia smell

and with no fuss, no announcement,
nothing left to say
she's suddenly gone
in a shower of purple rain.

Here they come now –
hotlips and fuschias,
salvias, anemones, nemesia,
roses trailing their

ordinary pinks –
and in her place a flame-tailed crocosmia
roosted by the wet stone wall;
the soundless stars.

A Fever Of Sunflowers

The first sign of sickness
a strange thirst for yellow
and the jealous hoarding of seeds,
till it's time to tear cobwebs from pots
for the birthing of sunflowers.

A yellow virus arrives
in the fields of my imagining –
a shot of honey under the skin,
incurable.

Day after day, month after month
hanging out with sunflowers,
my skin shining gold
watching with sunflower eyes
beetles in clover, a mouse running.

Deep in communion with these yellow nuns
through the green heat of summer
and the ice-rinks of winter

sick to the shrunken husks of them.

Lockdown Holiday

In this English field
the sunflowers are short like children
and have a holiday smell.

Word got around
and with nowhere to go
the day trippers came,
a worshipping hive of the dispossessed
swarming our small suns
with picnics and selfies –

everything that we were missing
found in this destination of sunflowers.

When all roads lead to nowhere
you can forget about roadmaps –
the only way out of here,
is here.

Sunflowers, Saumur

Leaving behind
the swimming pool shouts of the campsite
I take an old black hired bicycle
down country lanes, squeaking and
clonking through a song of bees

to a village lost in time –
old men with berets and hens,
wives silent behind Chantilly lace,
a white, stiff-shouldered signpost.

Under the blue helmet of sky
hunched regiments of sunflowers
are contemplating the wombless earth
into which they fell

and will fall again
and keep on falling
for eternity.

Life Of Clytie

What more could I do to prove my love –

nine days, stripped and starving on the hillside
and still Apollo was unfaithful – though it suited him
to keep me in thrall.

What's a girl to do when he makes of her
a prisoner inside a sunflower's body

forces her to watch adoringly and immortally
his shining infidelities.

The Psychology Of Sunflowers

Because we are born gold
you have made of us goddesses –
while our small hopes glitter and wither
through the unused hours.

For centuries we have practiced
rigid acquiescence, and learned to dream
only in yellow.

The Evening Primrose

In the daytime
I stand demurely by the gate
wilting in cow parsley.

Come dusk
drunk on my own sassy fragrance
I bare my seven yellow breasts
to the dark blue grass
and up to the stars.

The Russian Giant

She was light as a kitten,
perched on my shoulder for a better view
of a world no one had shown her –

reaching out for shining rowanberries
above the orphanage wall,
and in the sunken playground the brown rags
of an aquilegia;

even the manky dog beyond the gate;
these things made her happy –
but not the Russian giant.

She reared away from his fluttering arms
and his beaming sunny face –
dug her claws deep in my soul;

held fast to her unwritten stories
inside the book of love.

Miss Happiness

We found a sunflower head on the gatepost
a young one, carelessly murdered
bleeding a sticky substance
like liquid sellotape,
and that elusive smell –
honey, linen, birdwing, spice.

We named her Miss Happiness,
carried her home and set her to float
in a white bowl of water
where she could dream of her starry sisters
bowed and silent in the night field –

small grey hearts on a severed stem
cooling in moonlight.

Old Sunflowers

No one comes to see us
we, who were once goddesses –
suddenly old dames in hard hats.

We're exhausted by summer
and too much attention from the fickle crowd
that wanted only to bask in the
light of borrowed gold

not to sit with us in a boggy field
and hold our hands through
the coming storms.

We made for you a happy place,
a shelter from your human misery;
you can hide from our ravaged faces –
but you cannot hide from yourselves.

The young ones are out to dance
at the far side of the field
parading their joy like nightingales;
how long before they feel
the pinchy fingers of winter.

We, who remain constant,
are not like you; moving like shadows
towards all that is yielding,
and glowing.

Sunflowers In October

You'd think they were dressed for Halloween
in their dirty rags and hollow faces
row upon row of shrivelled sisters
in the white unholy light of a Sunday morning.

Here's an old one I remember well,
heavy with offspring and staring into
the half-forgotten earth –
does she remember who she was?

I lift her poor dead head that once
was the size of a steering wheel
and slowly begin to roll away seeds,
clumping like wet flies at her feet.

Peeling down to the orange membrane
I find the drowned lamps of summer
the undimmed lights of her –
a perfect glimmering summer ghost.

Optimism

Even now, we're stricken with the east
our shepherd-crook bodies gone to driftwood
our sunflower faces a hook of thistle.
Here's another winter sunset
unfriendly on our backs.

The evening sky, gold lights and indigo
has stolen our celebrity
and the big oak trees stained ochre;
but tomorrow, and tomorrow, and tomorrow
we will come back better than we are.

A New Wood Pigeon Tries Her Wings

two snaps
        then she summits
                      tilted on the blue edge
            of her rollercoaster
like the moment before
            the outbreath
      pushing us
on